What is hearing?

Molly Aloian

🌳 Crabtree Publishing Company
www.crabtreebooks.com

Author
Molly Aloian

Publishing plan research and development
Sean Charlebois, Reagan Miller
Crabtree Publishing Company

Editorial director
Kathy Middleton

Editor
Crystal Sikkens

Proofreader
Kelley McNiven

Design
Samara Parent

Photo research
Samara Parent

**Production coordinator
and prepress technician**
Samara Parent

Print coordinator
Katherine Berti

Illustrations
Bonna Rouse: page 17

Photographs
Thinkstock: pages 11 (top), 17 (left)
All other images by Shutterstock

Library and Archives Canada Cataloguing in Publication

Aloian, Molly
      What is hearing? / Molly Aloian.

(Senses close-up)
Includes index.
Issued also in electronic format.
ISBN 978-0-7787-0970-1 (bound).--ISBN 978-0-7787-0997-8 (pbk.)

      1. Hearing--Juvenile literature. I. Title. II. Series: Senses close-up

QP462.2.A56 2013   j612.8'5   C2013-901023-8

Library of Congress Cataloging-in-Publication Data

Aloian, Molly.
    What is hearing? / Molly Aloian.
       pages cm. -- (Senses close-up)
Audience: 5-8
Audience: K to grade 3
  Includes index.
  ISBN 978-0-7787-0970-1 (reinforced library binding) -- ISBN 978-0-7787-0997-8 (pbk.) -- ISBN 978-1-4271-9292-9 (electronic pdf) -- ISBN 978-1-4271-9216-5 (electronic html)
  1. Hearing--Juvenile literature. 2. Ear--Juvenile literature. 3. Senses and sensation--Juvenile literature. I. Title.

  QP462.2.A46 2013
  612.8'5--dc23
                                   2013004906

Crabtree Publishing Company

Printed in the U.S.A./042013/SX20130306

www.crabtreebooks.com   1-800-387-7650

**Published in Canada
Crabtree Publishing**
616 Welland Ave.
St. Catharines, Ontario
L2M 5V6

**Published in the United States
Crabtree Publishing**
PMB 59051
350 Fifth Avenue, 59th Floor
New York, New York 10118

**Published in the United Kingdom
Crabtree Publishing**
Maritime House
Basin Road North, Hove
BN41 1WR

**Published in Australia
Crabtree Publishing**
3 Charles Street
Coburg North
VIC 3058

Contents

Your sense of hearing

Hearing is one of your five main senses. Your other four senses are touch, taste, sight, and smell. You use all of your senses all of the time. Your senses help you learn about your surroundings.

taste

sight

hearing

touch

smell

You heard it here!

You hear sounds through your ears. You can hear loud sounds and quiet sounds. You can hear low sounds and high sounds. Take a moment to listen to the sounds around you right now. What do you hear?

Having an ear on each side of your head lets you hear sounds from all directions.

5

Parts of the ear

Your ears have three main parts. They are the outer ear, the middle ear, and the inner ear. All day long, your ears work together with your brain to hear sounds.

Sound waves

Sounds travel through the air as **sound waves**. Your outer ear catches sound waves and moves them into your **ear canal**. The ear canal leads to your eardrum. Your eardrum is a thin piece of skin inside your ear that **vibrates** when sound waves hit it.

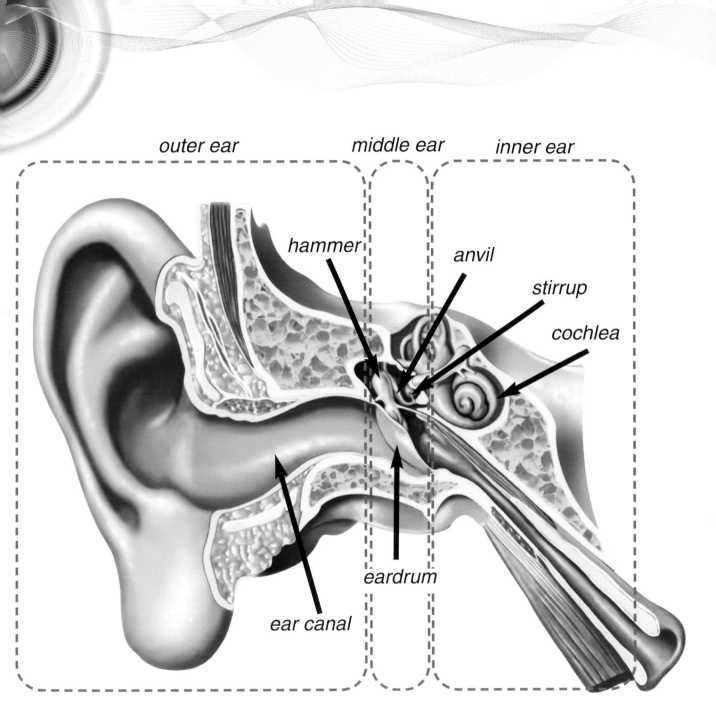

outer ear

middle ear

inner ear

hammer

anvil

stirrup

cochlea

eardrum

ear canal

How ears hear

As your eardrum vibrates, it moves three tiny bones in your middle ear. The bones are called the anvil, the hammer, and the stirrup. When these bones move, the vibrations move deeper into your ear.

Good vibrations

The vibrations travel into your inner ear until they reach a curly tube. This tube is called the cochlea. Tiny hairs on the cochlea move. The hairs are connected to **nerves**. The nerves send messages to your brain. Your brain then tells you what is making the sound.

What do you think?

If you place your hands over your ears, you cannot hear as well. Why do you think this is?

Types of sounds

Some sound waves move faster than others. Sound waves that move quickly have a high **pitch**. Whistles make high-pitched sounds. Baby birds chirping also make high-pitched sounds.

whistle

Get low

Sound waves that move slowly have a low pitch. A huge transport truck driving down the road makes a low-pitch sound.

jackhammer

tuba

fire alarm

lion roaring

What do you think?

Name three things on this page that make low-pitched sounds?

11

Hearing helps you

Your sense of hearing helps you learn about what is going on around you. You can hear your cat meow when he or she is hungry. You can hear your favorite song on the radio and sing along.

Hearing at school

At school, the sound of the bell tells you class is about to start. Your sense of hearing also helps you listen carefully to your teacher. In gym class, the sound of the whistle tells you to stop or start playing your game.

What do you think?

If your teacher raises his or her voice during class, what does it tell you? How do you react?

Staying safe

Your sense of hearing also helps you stay safe. You can hear noisy cars, trains, and buses and stay out of their way. If you get lost, you can hear an adult calling your name.

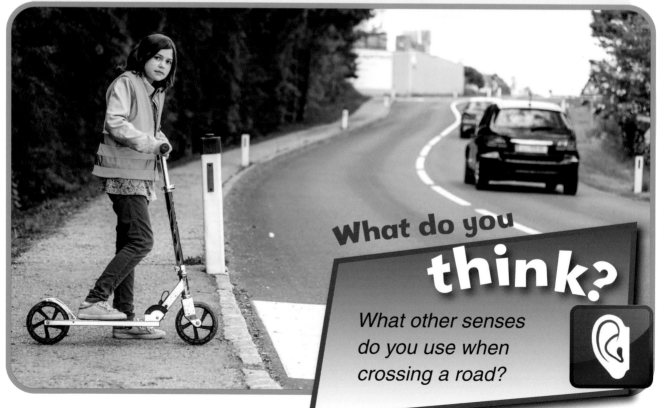

What do you think?

What other senses do you use when crossing a road?

Sirens and alarms

Loud sirens tell you that there is an emergency nearby. The sound of a smoke alarm tells you there might be a fire. Try to think of another warning sound and what that sound tells you.

siren

A fire truck's siren lets other drivers know to move out of the way so the fire truck can get to a fire quickly.

Animals hear, too

Just like people, animals use their sense of hearing all the time. A rabbit has long ears. It can hear when a **predator** is getting too close. A mother bird can hear her chicks chirping for food. This tells her to feed them.

A rabbit can turn its ears to hear sounds behind it.

Special hearing

Some animals, such as bats, use their hearing to find out what is around them. Bats make loud high-pitched cries. The sound waves from their cries bounce off objects around them and echo back. The bats hear the echoes and know what is nearby.

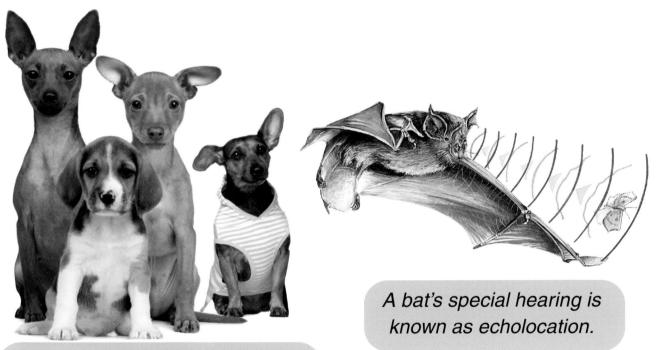

Dogs can also hear high-pitched sounds that people cannot hear.

A bat's special hearing is known as echolocation.

Help to hear

Some people are **deaf**. This means that they cannot hear any sounds, including other people's voices. People who are deaf can use **sign language** to "talk" with other people. Sign language is using your hands to make different signs. Different signs stand for different words.

"love"

"I love you"

"food"

Hearing loss

Some people might have damaged hearing or slowly lose their sense of hearing over time. These people need **hearing aids** to help them hear the sounds around them. Hearing aids make sounds louder.

hearing aid

Protect your hearing

Loud noises can damage your sense of hearing. It is important to wear earplugs if you attend loud music concerts or loud sporting events. The earplugs will keep loud sounds from entering your ears.

What do you think?

Name the senses you use when you are watching your favorite program on television. Name the senses you use when you play a musical instrument.

earplugs

Keep it low

When you hear your favorite song, you might want to turn up the volume. Listening to loud music can damage your hearing, however. Remember to always listen to music at a low volume.

21

What's that sound?

Have you ever used your sense of hearing to guess what is inside a gift box? You and a friend can try guessing what is inside a box by listening to the sounds the object makes. You will need:

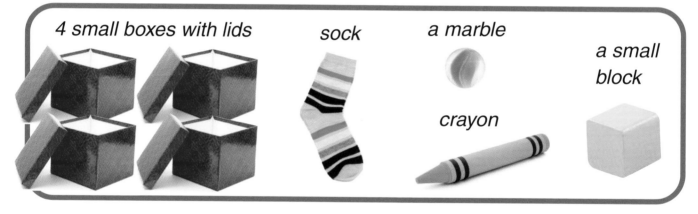

4 small boxes with lids

sock

a marble

crayon

a small block

1. Show your friend the four objects.
2. Ask your friend to close their eyes.
3. Put an object in each of the boxes.
4. Have your friend handle the boxes and describe what sounds the objects are making.
5. Ask your friend to guess which object is in each box.

Did he or she guess correctly? Why or why not? Do the same activity with different objects and record your results.

Learning more

Books

What is Hearing? (Lightning Bolt Books: Your Amazing Senses) by Jennifer Boothroyd. Lerner Publications, 2012.

Amazing Sound (Amazing Science) by Sally Hewitt. Crabtree Publishing Company, 2007.

My Senses Help Me (My World) by Bobbie Kalman. Crabtree Publishing Company, 2010.

Sound and Hearing (Science Corner) by Angela Royston. Powerkids Press, 2011.

Websites

The Sense of Hearing
www.wisc-online.com/objects/ViewObject.aspx?ID=AP14204

All About Your Senses: Experiments to Try
http://kidshealth.org/kid/closet/experiments/experiment_main.html

Sid the Science Kid
http://pbskids.org/sid/isense.html

Hearing Facts
http://idahoptv.org/dialogue4kids/season8/hearing/facts.cfm

Words to know

deaf (def) adjective Not able to hear

ear canal (eer kuh-NAL) noun The narrow tunnel-like part of your ear that leads to your eardrum

hearing aid (HEER-ing eyd) noun A special device that make sounds louder

nerves (nurvs) noun Thin strings of tissue; nerves carry messages from your brain to other parts of your body

pitch (pich) noun The highness or lowness of a sound

predator (PRED-uh-ter) noun An animal that hunts and eats other animals

sound waves (sound weyvs) noun Vibrations that enter the ear that are heard as sounds

sign language (sahyn LANG-gwij) noun A way for deaf people to communicate with hand movements

vibrate (VAHY-breyt) verb To move quickly backward and forward

*A noun is a person, place, or thing.
An adjective is a word that tells you what something is like.
A verb is an action word that tells you what someone or something does.*

Index